→ HOW LONG DOES A REDWOOD TREE LIVE?

BY EMILY HUDD

CONTENT CONSULTANT

Kevin O'Hara, PhD, Professor, Department of
Environmental Science, Policy, and Management,
University of California, Berkeley

CAPSTONE PRESS
a capstone imprint

Fact Finders Books are published by Capstone Press,
1710 Roe Crest Drive, North Mankato, Minnesota 56003
www.mycapstone.com

Library of Congress Cataloging-in-Publication Data
Names: Hudd, Emily, author.
Title: How long does a redwood tree live? / by Emily Hudd.
Description: North Mankato, Minnesota : Capstone Press, [2020] | Series: How
   long does it take? | Includes bibliographical references and index.
Identifiers: LCCN 2019000187 (print) | LCCN 2019003574 (ebook) | ISBN
   9781543573015 (ebook) | ISBN 9781543572957 (hardcover) | ISBN
   9781543575408 (paperback)
Subjects: LCSH: Redwoods--Juvenile literature. | Redwoods--Life
   cycles--Juvenile literature.
Classification: LCC QK494.5.T3 (ebook) | LCC QK494.5.T3 H83 2020 (print) |
   DDC 585/.5--dc23
LC record available at https://lccn.loc.gov/2019000187

All internet sites appearing in back matter were available and accurate when this book was sent to press.

Editorial Credits
Editor: Marie Pearson
Designer and production specialist: Dan Peluso

Photo Credits
Alamy: blickwinkel/Jagel, 7, 23 (top right); iStockphoto: benedek, cover; Kevin L. O'Hara: 11, 18–19; Science Source: Gregory G. Dimijian, M.D., 17, 23 (bottom right); Shutterstock Images: Ethan Daniels, 13, Leonard Zhukovsky, 28, Mariusz S. Jurgielewicz, 24–25, MNStudio, 20, My Good Images, 29, Robert Mutch, 14, Robert Mutch, 26, Sundry Photography, 10, 23 (bottom left), Vahan Abrahamyan, 8, 23 (top left), Wollertz, 5

Design Elements: Red Line Editorial

Printed in the United States of America.
PA70

TABLE OF
CONTENTS

HIKING WITH GIANTS

Two friends hike through a forest on the coast of California. They look up at the giant trees surrounding them. The trees' branches begin hundreds of feet from the ground. The sunlight shines dimly through the leaves. The red-brown bark is scruffy. The friends know these majestic trees have been around for hundreds or even thousands of years.

Redwoods are conifer trees. Conifer trees produce cones that contain seeds. Redwoods are also evergreens. Evergreens keep their leaves all year long. Their leaves are different from other trees.

They are usually thicker. They might be needle-like. Evergreen leaves can live through all the seasons of the year. Redwoods live a long time. The oldest coast redwood is 2,520 years old. That means it started growing in 480 BC.

Many people enjoy visiting redwood forests.

CHAPTER ONE

STARTING SMALL

Some redwoods grow from seeds. Seeds grow in cones on the trees. Cones can be male or female. They grow on the same tree. Male cones produce pollen. Female cones need pollen for their seeds to develop. The cones **flower** between February and May. Female cones grow on the top branches. Male cones develop on the lower branches. Wind carries the pollen upward. The pollen reaches the flowering female cones and helps them make seeds. Seeds take two years to develop.

FACT One redwood can make more than 100,000 seeds in a year.

flower—to blossom and produce cones and seeds

Cones grow near the ends of a redwood's branches.

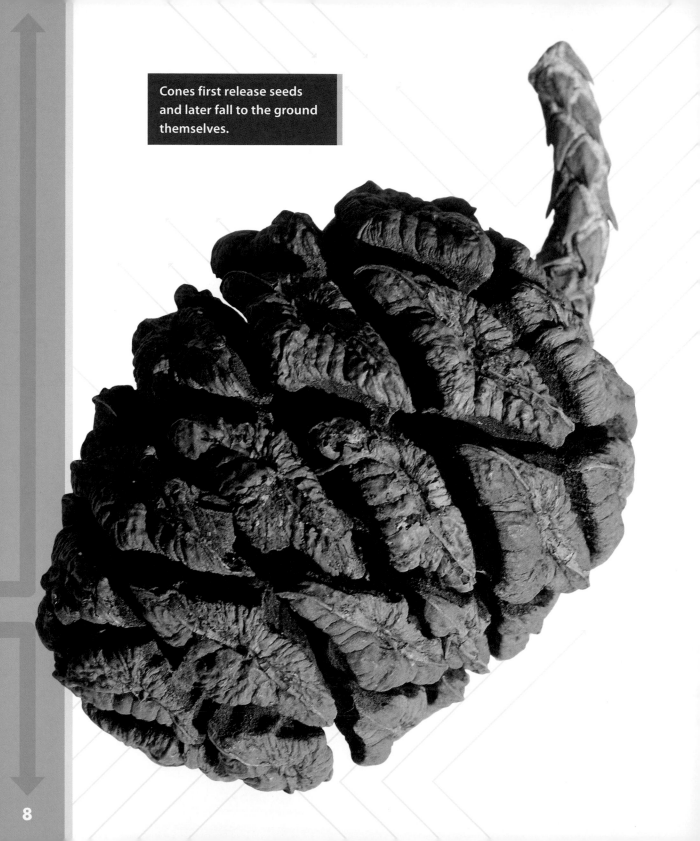

Cones first release seeds and later fall to the ground themselves.

Redwoods as young as 24 years old can produce cones if they have lots of sunlight. The seeds are shed before the cone falls. The seeds **disperse** in many ways. They can fall to the ground. Wind can move them. Birds or animals may carry them to new places.

Seeds on the ground need wet soil and sunlight to grow. Most seeds do not **germinate**. Many are infertile, meaning they cannot sprout. Or the soil might be too dry. There may be too much shade from large trees for the new seedling to get started. For all these reasons, many redwoods begin to grow another way.

disperse—**to scatter**

germinate—**begin to grow**

Sprouts can grow from a fallen log.

Redwoods can also **regenerate** from sprouts at the base of a tree. This is how most redwood trees begin. Sprouts often form at the base of the tree trunk. They

> **FACT**
> Redwoods can sprout from burls too. Burls are knotty growths on the trunk.

can form on roots and cut stumps. They can grow on a cut log or from high on the tree stem after a fire.

regenerate—to make new

FAIRY RINGS

Sometimes a circle of sprouts forms around a cut stump of a tree. The sprouts start to grow. Some die off. Others grow stronger. Eventually, the original tree dies or is cut down. But the young circle of sprouts is still alive. The circle is called a fairy ring.

The sprout is attached to the original tree's roots. It shares the same **nutrients** and water that the tree used to grow. It doesn't have to worry about finding wet soil or lots of sunlight. This is probably how many redwoods originated.

Sprouts may grow into a ring of trees around a stump.

nutrient—a food or element living things need to grow

CHAPTER TWO

YOUNG REDWOODS

A belt of redwoods grows in California. It is near the Pacific Ocean. The belt is 450 miles (720 kilometers) long. It is less than 30 miles (50 km) wide. The redwoods need lots of water in their **habitat**. The rainy season is from October to April. In that time, the main part of the redwood belt gets 60 inches (150 centimeters) or more of rain.

FACT Most redwoods grow less than 40 miles (65 km) from the ocean.

In summer, fog often covers the coast. It helps redwoods survive. Redwoods get 40 percent of their water from fog during the summer months.

habitat—the environment where an animal or plant lives

Fog in redwood forests is common during summer.

Fog naturally cools the hot summer air. It also provides extra water for the trees. Water droplets bead up on leaves. Redwoods can draw water from the leaves. Some water drips to the forest floor. The trees' roots soak up water from the soil too.

Redwood leaves are narrow and pointed. Some are flat.

Redwood growth depends on the weather. The trees use sunlight as energy to grow. In the right conditions, they can grow up to 5 feet (1.5 meters) in one year! Sometimes they are stressed from lack of water or sunlight. They might only grow 1 inch (2.5 cm) the whole year.

Redwoods make different leaves as they grow. Leaves at the top of the tree are more like needles. They are tight spikes. They hold in water. This shape protects the leaf from light and heat. It helps keep the redwood from getting **dehydrated**. Leaves on the lower part of the tree are flat. They need to be wider to catch sunlight.

dehydrated—lacking the necessary amount of water needed to survive

CHAPTER THREE

HUGE TREES

Redwoods grow taller than any other tree species in the world. Redwoods can reach 200 to 240 feet (60 to 75 m) tall. The trunk is 10 to 15 feet (3 to 4.5 m) wide. The tallest redwoods are more than 360 feet (110 m) tall. That is as long as a football field!

A redwood has a strong trunk. It has to support the tall tree. The bark is soft but thick. It is 6 to 12 inches (15 to 30 cm) thick on older trees. The tree is named for its color. This red-brown color fades over time. Old redwoods have bark that looks gray.

FACT

The tallest redwood is more than 380 feet (115 m) tall. It's named Hyperion.

Redwoods tower above most other trees.

The trunk has layers. Each year, a tree adds a layer of wood. Water, sunlight, and the warming weather in spring help the tree grow. The wood grown in spring is lighter because it grows quickly. The wood grown in summer is darker. Growth slows down as the weather gets warmer. These changes create a pattern of light and dark rings. The age of trees can be found by counting the rings on a stump after it falls or is cut down.

Tree rings can show how many years the tree has been growing. They can also show what the tree's life was like. Thick rings grow during years with plenty of water and sunshine. Thin rings mean the tree was stressed. Rings can also show when fires occurred or when an animal damaged the tree.

Rings

Redwoods have shallow roots for their size. They do not go deep into the ground. Instead, they spread wide in all directions. They have to find enough nutrients and water to support the huge tree.

A redwood's roots are underground. Sometimes the roots connect with the roots of nearby trees.

DOUGLAS-FIRS

Douglas-firs are another very tall tree. They have gray bark. They can grow 295 feet (90 m) tall. Some Douglas-firs grow in the same areas as redwoods.

When the roots spread out, they may connect to roots of nearby redwoods. This makes all the trees stronger. They are linked together, and they share nutrients. They stay standing after strong winds and floods.

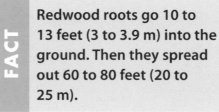

FACT

Redwood roots go 10 to 13 feet (3 to 3.9 m) into the ground. Then they spread out 60 to 80 feet (20 to 25 m).

Redwoods need other trees, plants, and animals to survive. A healthy redwood forest has **diversity**. Redwoods get nutrients from bushes and plants. This includes mosses and mushrooms, which help nourish the soil.

diversity—**having a variety of different things or traits**

CHAPTER FOUR

DEATH

Redwoods can live for 600 years. Some live for more than 2,000 years. But people may also add a sprout's age to the age of its parent tree. A sprout can be considered the same tree as the one it grew from. A tree alive today may be the continuation of a tree that grew many thousands of years ago.

GIANT SEQUOIAS

Giant sequoias are incredible trees that can live even longer than redwoods. Sequoias can live more than 3,000 years. They are also evergreen trees that germinate from seeds from cones. Sequoias grow in California at high elevations. Their trunks can grow thicker than redwoods, but they don't grow as tall.

The coast redwood species has existed since the time of the dinosaurs. Fossil records show redwoods from 160 million years ago. This shows the species' ability to survive over time.

Seeds take two years to develop.

It takes 24 years before the tree produces cones.

Sprouts form on the fallen tree after 2 or 3 weeks.

The tree dies after about 600 years, though some live longer than 2,000 years.

Natural threats to redwood trees include fire, insects, and disease. Fire can burn and damage the trunk. It can cause the tree to collapse. Some insects eat trees. Diseases can affect tree growth. All these can damage or weaken trees. But insects and disease are not big threats to redwoods.

hollow—**an unfilled space**

Sometimes bats live in redwood hollows.

Redwoods are not easily damaged. Tannin is a chemical in redwood bark that protects trees from insects and disease. Redwoods' thick bark protects them during fires. On older trees, the leaves and branches begin high above the ground. Only flames in severe fires reach them. But fire is more of a threat to smaller redwoods.

Coast redwood logs provide a habitat for many other plants and animals.

Death is a natural part of the life cycle of redwoods. The tree **decomposes**. Dead trees add nutrients to the soil. Other trees use the nutrients to grow. However, the life cycle of redwood trees has changed over time.

decompose—**to break down into smaller pieces**

Logging of redwoods began in the 1850s. That is when California became a U.S. state. After a massive earthquake hit San Francisco, California, in 1906, logging increased. People needed wood to rebuild homes.

Logging affects the life cycle of redwoods. It does not let trees come to a natural death. It cuts them down before they fall to the ground. This takes away the nutrients the dead tree could give to the soil.

FACT Before Europeans arrived, some American Indians lived in redwood forests. The Yurok used fallen redwoods to make their homes.

Today, many people want to help redwoods. Redwood parks in California protect the trees from logging. The parks also have trails. People can follow the trails through redwood forests. At the same time, trails protect the trees from soil compaction. Soil compaction happens when people stand around tree trunks and pack down the soil. This harms the soil and the tree's ability to get the nutrients it needs.

Muir Woods is a popular park with redwoods.

MUIR WOODS NATIONAL MONUMENT
UNITED STATES DEPARTMENT OF THE INTERIOR
NATIONAL PARK SERVICE

Trails help keep redwoods safe.

Some people grow redwoods in **nurseries**. The seeds are planted and taken care of. Once a tree starts growing, it is replanted in the forest. Nurseries aim to increase the redwood population.

Redwoods can live for 2,000 years. They can grow more than 350 feet (100 m) tall. People today can see and touch trees older than any person on Earth.

FACT
Several parks in California have redwoods. There is even a national park dedicated to the trees. Redwood National Park opened in 1968.

nursery—a place where people grow plants from seeds

GLOSSARY

decompose (dee-kum-POZE)—to break down into smaller pieces

dehydrated (dee-HYE-dray-tid)—lacking the necessary amount of water needed to survive

disperse (dis-PURS)—to scatter

diversity (di-VUR-si-tee)—having a variety of different things or traits

flower (FLOU-ur)—to blossom and produce cones and seeds

germinate (JUR-muh-nate)—begin to grow

habitat (HA-bi-tat)—the environment where an animal or plant lives

hollow (HAH-loh)—an unfilled space

nursery (NUR-sur-ee)—a place where people grow plants from seeds

nutrient (NOO-tree-uhnt)—a food or element living things need to grow

regenerate (ree-JEN-uh-rate)—to make new

ADDITIONAL RESOURCES

FURTHER READING

Cosson, M.J. *Welcome to Redwood National and State Parks*. Visitor Guides. Mankato, Minn.: Child's World, 2018.

Hickey, Cat. *Forest*. DK Find Out! New York: DK Publishing, 2017.

Jiménez, Vita. *We Need Trees! Caring for Our Planet*. Me, My Friends, My Community. Minneapolis, Minn.: Cantata Learning, 2017.

Kirchner, Jason. *California*. States. North Mankato, Minn: Capstone Press, 2017.

CRITICAL THINKING QUESTIONS

1. In your own words, describe how redwoods grow and how temperature and weather can affect them. Use evidence from the text to support your answer.

2. Redwoods can live for thousands of years. How do they survive for so long?

3. What is one way redwoods and giant sequoias are similar? What is one way they are different?

INTERNET SITES

DK Find Out! Evergreen Trees
https://www.dkfindout.com/us/animals-and-nature/plants/evergreen-trees/

National Geographic Kids: Redwood National and State Parks
https://kids.nationalgeographic.com/explore/nature/redwoodnationalandstateparks/#redwood-forest.jpg

National Park Service Kids: Redwood
https://www.nps.gov/redw/learn/kidsyouth/index.htm

INDEX

ABOUT THE AUTHOR

Emily Hudd is a full-time children's author who loves writing nonfiction on a variety of topics. She lives in Minnesota with her husband.